Tom and Kate Go to Westminster

CHILDREN'S REVOLT
COLOURED VERSION

CHILDREN SAVING OUR PLANET SERIES

CAROL SUTTERS

Illustrated by William Fong

AuthorHouse™ UK
1663 Liberty Drive
Bloomington, IN 47403 USA
www.authorhouse.co.uk
UK TFN: 0800 0148641 (Toll Free inside the UK)
UK Local: 02036 956322 (+44 20 3695 6322 from outside the UK)

This book is printed on acid-free paper.

ISBN: 978-1-6655-8601-6 (sc)
ISBN: 978-1-6655-8600-9 (e)

Print information available on the last page.

Published by AuthorHouse 03/24/2021

authorHOUSE®

Mum said, "We are going out on a long journey by bus to the Houses of Parliament to see the crowd of school children which will gather there today."

"Why are they going there?", asks Kate.

Mum says, "To ask the adults who rule the country to preserve our planet earth and not destroy it so that it will be safe for you when you get older."

"These rulers are called politicians and meet at The Houses of Parliament in London. Politicians make laws which people and businesses have to follow."

Tom and Kate and their Mum travel by bus to Westminster. It is a long journey and on the way lots of school children also board the bus with banners and signs and make it very cramped.

Outside the Houses of Parliament there are lots of children standing with boards and banners shouting *"Save our Planet."*

Mum says, *"The Children have not gone to school today in order to travel here to ask the politicians to take action to save planet earth and not cause damage to it by lots of things we currently do."*

"Children have realised that there is now a climate emergency and we need the politicians to make laws for action to be taken quickly. Children understand that some of the actions and laws humans make destroy the natural world that supports us and we need to stop this."

"The children want these politicians to make new laws like ones to make us all try harder to stop using plastic bottles which hurt sea creatures, or to use cars less which uses less fuel that causes pollution, and to fly less in aeroplanes."

Tom says, "*We are already doing some of these things Mum, aren't we?*"

"*Yes*", says Mum.

"*We are trying to take steps to go more green to preserve our planet earth and allow all the animals and plants to live happily with us humans. We must not harm animals and plants or kill them off as we need them for the future survival of all of us on planet earth.*"

When the children returned home Mum said to them, "*Look we were televised on The News as hundreds of children around the country also travelled to London to join together to protest in a march outside The Houses of Parliament.*"

Mum said, *"This was a very important day today as the children have sent a message that they want the planet with all its plants and animals to be loved and preserved."*

What did we learn today? (tick the box if you understood and agree)

☐ Children of today want to save the planet and all its animals and plants so that they can also enjoy them when they are older.

☐ If we destroy the natural habitat of plants and animals on earth and pollute the air, soil and water we will destroy our planet earth where we live.

☐ Children in the UK decided to protest and ask adults who rule the land and bosses of large companies to take action to stop this destruction.

☐ Children have realised there is a climate emergency.

Read what Kate and Tom did next in book 2.

Children Saving our Planet Series

Books

1. Tom and Kate Go to Westminster CHILDREN'S REVOLT

2. Kate and Tom Learn About Fossil Fuels

3. Tom and Kate Chose Green Carbon

4. Tress and Deforestation

5. Our Neighbourhood Houses

6. Our Neighbourhood Roads

7. Shopping at the Farm Shop

8. Travelling to a Holiday by the Sea

9. Picnic at the Seaside on Holiday

These series of simple books explain the landmark importance of Children's participation in the Extinction rebellion protest. Children actively want to encourage and support adults to urgently tackle both the Climate and the Biodiversity emergencies. The booklets enable children at an early age to understand some of the scientific principles that are affecting the destruction of the planet. If global political and economic systems fail to address the climate emergency, the responsibility will rest upon children to save the Planet for themselves.

This series is dedicated to

Theodore, Aria and Ophelia